The Consecration Of Banners

Thomas Pentycross

In the interest of creating a more extensive selection of rare historical book reprints, we have chosen to reproduce this title even though it may possibly have occasional imperfections such as missing and blurred pages, missing text, poor pictures, markings, dark backgrounds and other reproduction issues beyond our control. Because this work is culturally important, we have made it available as a part of our commitment to protecting, preserving and promoting the world's literature. Thank you for your understanding.

THE PRAYER.

O ALMIGHTY Lord God, the protector of all that trust in thee, who hast formed all things living with a feeling of self-defence, vouchsafe, we beseech thee, to bless the arms which thy servant our Sovereign hath put into our hands, for the preservation of peace and order about our dwellings. Lift up the light of thy countenance over the King and Kingdom, the Church of the realm and the Church universal, and over all orders and degrees of men amongst us. Have respect unto our fleets and armies, and receive our thanksgivings for the many and great victories thou hast been pleased to afford us. Accept and bless the armed Associations of the Land, whose spirits thou hast stirred up for the preservation of our Laws, Liberty, Property, Lives, and Religion: and more particularly we pray for the armed Association of this town, and for that of the neighbourhood here assisting us.

[8]

Pray we likewise for thine handmaid, the honourable woman who is about to present to us the Standard now laid at the foot of thy divine Majesty. Let thine altar sanctify the gift. Be it holiness unto thee. Yet, O Lord, remove, we beseech thee, all occasion of using it in fight. Hasten the time when we shall no longer hear the sound of the trumpet, the alarm of war; but sit every man under his vine, and under his fig-tree, in righteousness and peace.

These, and all mercies for ourselves and for all mankind, we humbly ask in the name and words of Jesus Christ our Lord.

Our Father, &c.

PSALM XX. 5.

IN THE NAME OF OUR GOD WILL WE SET UP OUR BANNERS.

NOTHING can be more coincident than this Psalm with this solemnity. What does it contain? The Church praying for its visible head, the King, at a time of great public alarm: the Church consecrating the banners of the state; " in the name of our God " will we set up our Banners;" disclaiming all trust in instruments of war, as chariots and horses, the great dependence of the enemy: then in faith " calling," like God himself, " things which are not as though they were;" and singing the ἐπινίκιον, or hymn of victory, as though the battle were finished before it was begun: she then closes all with prayer; " Save, Lord, the King*; hear us when we " call upon thee."

---

* So it should be translated: יהוה העשיעה המלך.

More particularly the Text excites *three ideas:* first, the Sanctification of Military Standards: secondly, Dependence upon God: and thirdly, Engagement in his Cause.

First, the Sanctification of Military Standards. But here Scrupulosity seizes our reins, stops our progress, and asks; Whether man, like God, can confer sanctity, and that on irrational and inanimate substance? Whether priests by ceremony can attach victory, or impart virtue, to Colours, as by magnetic sympathy or solemn incantation? Whether, departed long since as we have been from superstition, and gone over, perhaps, to an opposite extreme, we are returning, like a pendulum, whence we set out? Peace to the childish panic! All is sober, plain, useful, necessary; nothing fantastical, nothing superstitious, nothing pompous, in dedicating all we are and have to God; and particularly in dedicating to him *military apparatus,* of which the standard is a symbol. Is it not *merely decent* to lay the standard at the foot of Deity, for His acceptance and blessing? Is it not *highly important* to make it no longer vulgar, but " holiness to the Lord;" the standard above every thing?

First,

First, because, as human blood, that of one man is too sacred to be shed by magistracy itself without licence from God; so, much less may the blood of thousands be shed, the effect of war, without manifest commission from the same Lord of Life and Death.

To appropriate the Colours to God imports then, that they can never afterwards be used profanely; that is, wantonly or hastily: only by that light of reason, justice, and necessity, which are His *precept and warrant:* never from revenge, never from ambition, never from a lust of accumulating wealth, or propagating dominion.

Secondly, the sanctification of the Flag makes it the duty, on a *new account*, of all who enlist under it, to do and suffer any thing, not shrinking from death itself, that may occur in this line of service. We are never to see the *hallowed ensign*, without reflecting, " Thy vows are upon me, O God." To fight is no longer optionable, but a *sacred* as well as civil obligation: or, as the Romans called the oath to their Generals, *a sacrament*.

[12]

Here Pity still sighs as she remembers the brave and pious Gardiner, who at the battle of *Preston-Pans* stood alone, and, rather than fly, from conscience was cut in pieces.

Thirdly, the Banner is a token of Order, and a publication of the cause or country we defend. Without this instrument, Soldiers are a banditti by land, and Sailors pirates by sea. Be this representation, therefore, of law, in contradistinction to one of riot and rebellion, consecrated, and you proclaim yourselves religiously sons of the state, conservators of the peace; nay more, confessors and martyrs for Government and for God.

Fourthly, the Standard is not merely the rallying point of an army, but a specification of particular divisions in it. The instrument before us is an armorial picture of this ancient town, considered as coming forth in behalf of its own families, as well as for the general welfare. Not unlike the military arrangement of the Jews; where indeed were three tribes, with their respective distinctions, stationed on each of the four sides of the camp: but besides these, " every man " of the children of Israel was to pitch by
" his

" his own standard, with the ensign of his
" *father's house,*" some heraldic emblem of a
nearer and more affecting kind than that of
the tribe at large to which he belonged. Here
then are we with the scutcheon, not merely
of the kingdom or country, but of our father's
house; and its quarterings our kindred and
neighbours. The Standard shews us pledged
for a most precious and tender stake, that of
the peace, property, and lives of those who
are dear to us as ourselves. Let the Standard, then, be sanctified, unless you do not
wish to interest God on their behalf: or unless you can think with less pleasure of the
Standard of your father's and neighbour's
house, for being surrendered in form to God,
and made holiness to Him: or unless no new
motive to protect them can arise from the
consideration, that you are solemnly bound
for their defence, not merely by instinct or
benevolence, but in the faith and fear of
God.

The consecrated Banner fixes in us all
these ideas.

II. But the expression of the Text suggests

something else besides consecration; namely, Dependence upon God.

Independence of God, and sufficiency to ourselves for happiness without God, are the very soul of sin; its definition and idea. And what an instance of this essence of all evil is something not generally suspected by us: I mean an Epicurean proneness to suppose, that God leaves events to second causes. For example: We are apt to think a Cornwallis by land, or an Howe, a St. Vincent, a Duncan, or a Nelson, by sea, make victory a thing of course. But the history of all ages shews, what Religion is pleased with hearing our gallant Commanders confess, that the race is not to the swift, nor the battle to the strong; but the fate of fleets and armies hangeth on Him, whose style and title is the Lord of Hosts.

So we read in the sacred records, that, when Zerah the Ethiopian came with a million in his train against Asa, King of Judah, the good King abandons himself to God in faith and prayer, and presently Victory is dispatched to him from Heaven; and Fear, Rout, Flight,

Flight, Massacre, Spoil, annihilate the countless Ethiopian forces.

When Sennacherib (as an Heathen tells the story) with an immense army entered Egypt against Sethon its King, the result, we should all have predicted, must be Sethon's fall. For his officers and soldiers, whom he had long insulted, refused to march; only an handful of labourers from the shops, and peasants from the fields, followed him, obliged as he was, by command of Vulcan, still to proceed against Sennacherib. Sethon reaches the camp at Pelusium, surely to be devoured by it. Just the reverse. On the very night of his arrival were gnawn in pieces all the bowstrings of the enemy, so that they could not act *offensively*; and all the thongs of their shields, so that they could not act *defensively*: and thus, without bloodshed or trouble, did the few and the weak conquer the many and the strong. Holy Scripture applies this story to Hezekiah, and says, that "it came to pass "that night the angel of the LORD smote in "the camp of the Assyrians an hundred and "fourscore and five thousand*.

* Sir Isaac Newton, in his Chronology, reconciles Herodotus with the account given of this affair in
2 Kings.

The whole frame of human events moveth, like the four wheels of Ezekiel, whithersoever the Deity within conducts it: but particularly do the affairs of war receive their line of direction from Him. The weather and countless accidents without, all precarious; and skill, faith, courage, stratagem within, all precarious; are part of the vast apparatus, with which God obtains with ease His own counsels. He that pierced through the masonry, and entered the room where the doors were bolted and the windows barred, for fear of the Jews, admits himself, how readily, into all the fortunes of his creatures.

---

2 Kings xviii. First: *Mice*, which are said to have gnawn in pieces the bow-strings and thongs of the shields, were a common emblem of *destruction* among the Egyptians. Secondly: " By comparing 2 Kings " xviii. 21. with xix. 9. it is probable, that when Sen- " nacherib heard of the kings of Egypt and Ethiopia " coming against him, he went from Libnah towards " Pelusium, to oppose them, and was there surprised " and set upon in the night by them both, and routed " with as great a slaughter as if the bowstrings, &c. of " the Assyrians had been eaten by mice."—The great slaughter is expressed *hieroglyphically* by a multitude of mice entering and destroying the camp of Sennacherib.

Who should be the governor of the world but its Maker? It is good sense and policy, as well as piety then, to say, *In the name of our God*, in dependence upon Him, *will we set up our Banners!* By the way, what reason have we of this happy Island to trust in God, when we find him appearing for us in deliverance after deliverance, a long and illustrious procession; crowned, as they all have been, by the stupendous victory on the coast of Egypt! The mouth of the Nile speaks, and the Mediterranean reflects the voice, that *the Lord of hosts is with us*, that the *God of Jacob*, the God who hears and answers prayer, is *on our side*. Nay, scarcely have our astonished ears ceased ringing with *these* tidings, but, as if Deep calleth unto Deep every where on our behalf, the Irish sea bears the same loud testimony of *Emmanuel, God with us*.

A third idea suggested by the passage before us is, that the cause, in which we are engaged, is the cause of God: *in His name*, or on his account, we set *up our Banners*.

The religion of France is that of a ROBESPIERRE, in preference to that of JESUS CHRIST.—Who does not shudder? Who does not smile?—It is a religion *without a Deity*[*]: what a solecism!—It is a religion, of which Philosophy itself is ashamed; a religion of *abstract ideas*; such as Reason, Liberty, Nature, which, every body knows, have no personality, no individual subsistence of their own; but are perfect non-entities. This man reasons, that man is free; and the material world is subject to physical laws. But no such *beings* exist as Reason, as Liberty, as Nature. Be this however as it may; we shudder, but do not interfere. But when a *conspiracy* comes out to *crush the* WRETCH, as Jesus Christ is blasphemously called: and when it appears, that the projected overthrow of all governments has for its object, the robbing mankind of the belief of a God; our cause immediately becomes His. Should we be made the victims of French ambition, no Bible must be seen, no worship exist. If indeed religion has been at all endured in the conquered countries, it is only for the present;

[*] It was indeed put to the vote, and carried by Robespierre, that there should be a Deity: but all the world knows this was a mere stroke of policy, suited to the prejudices of the vulgar, and that atheism is the real creed of the Directory, and of all their party, and the creed intended to be taught every where by their agents. *Buonaparte* invokes *Fortune*.

till,

till, by the diffusion of their principles, and establishment of their power, the very semblance and even remembrance of such a thing as religion is extirpated there, and throughout the earth.

* *Ask then of the days that are past, which were before thee, since the day that God created man upon the earth: and ask from the one side of heaven unto the other, whether there hath been any such great thing as this is, or hath been heard like it*; a plot of such enormous wickedness: and whether a greater occasion can occur for man (I had almost added woman, and child) to say, *In the name of our God will we set up our banners.* I recal that *almost*; for it is women, and only women, and honourable women, who here, and throughout the kingdom, provide banners, and put them into your hands. Female fear and delicacy forgets, on this occasion, its wonted love of blushing retirement, feels manly fortitude, and comes forth at the head of armed troops, to adjure you, never to fully by negligence, cowardice, or other abuse, the colours it presents; but to receive them as extraordinary pledges to your

---

* Deuteronomy iv. 32.

country, for courage, faith, and every the moſt ſtrenuous exertion.

In the mean time, *Principalities and Powers of darkneſs*, the Goſpel of Jeſus Chriſt defies you. That auguſt and holy matron, the Church univerſal, ſhakes her head at you, and, *with Him who ſitteth in heaven, laughs you to ſcorn*. Annihilate Chriſtianity! Try firſt to depopulate heaven, and expunge creation. Your poiſon ſhall become medicine to the Church; your rage againſt it ſhall be its propagation, its perfection, its glory. Your earthquakes, that overthrow mountains, ſhall only fill up valleys, to make an immenſe level for the grand Millennial Car of the Son of God.

Is your patience exhauſted? Is your candor weary? If not, ſuffer me to take occaſion, from the *plurality* of Banners in the text, to hold up *one* to you, very different in kind, though perfectly coincident in deſign, with that which is there waving. It is one of infinitely greater worth than the fate of kingdoms, or the mere lives of all human-kind. It is one, which, if you value yourſelves as well as others, you will behold with rapture and worſhip. This earth exhibits nothing

like

like it; and heaven itself, nothing superior to it. It is that, which God himself cannot surpass; I mean, the CROSS *of our Lord Jesus Christ:* who, says Isaiah, shall be lifted up as an *ensign* to the nations, and to whom, says Moses, shall the gathering of the people be.

Know ye this, all ye people, that sinful creatures as we are, conceived and born in iniquity, the tender mercy of our God, not willing *that any should perish, but that all should come to repentance*, hath provided a great and divine Saviour, who *made himself a sin-offering for us; who gave his life a ransom for us; who hath finished transgression; made an end of sin; made reconciliation for iniquity; and brought in an everlasting righteousness.* And now the standard of pardon and eternal life is lifted up in JESUS; *look to him* then, *and be saved, all the ends of the earth.* Let none exclude themselves: for Jesus Christ excludes none but those, *who will not come to Him, that they may have life.*

The magnificent and divine undertaking of Jesus Christ is,

To receive with open arms all of humankind, in all ages, who, conscious of their guilt and corruption, only apply to him for pardon and purification:

To exempt them *immediately* from most exquisite and everlasting punishment, the just doom of sin:

To mortify in them *now* every thing of the nature of bad and wrong; and at length, in another world, to extirpate in them the being, the imagination, and even the capacity of evil:

To adorn and fill them with all moral beauty and excellence, here *initially*, hereafter *perfectly*:

To turn all the afflictions of this life into blessings; and all its comforts into preludes to eternal comforts:

To bestow and charge upon them the liberty and dignity of serving God, in all the offices of religion, and in all the good works attached to their various stations and relations in life:

To restore their bodies from the grave, and to crown them with ineffable youth, lustre, and glory, as fit vehicles for their immaculate and perfect souls:

To make them, not prisoners, but, assessors with Him at the universal judgment:

To exalt them to serve God, face to face, around His throne:

To fix them in the region of bliss, of goodness, and of glory: and there

To *eternize* them in intimate union and plenary communion with the all-sufficient and inexhaustible DEITY *Himself*.

Is this the design and engagement of Jesus Christ, to all who flee to Him for refuge? God enable us then with pleasure, speed, penitence, and faith, to resort to the Banner of this stupendous Redeemer, and be made for ever!

Again. Because in the discipline of Jesus Christ, cleansing us from evil, and consummating good in us, great and many are the temptations which will occur; dreadful the ingenuity,

genuity, assiduity, and power of the author and support of sin, and most infirm the human heart; another Standard is displayed, on the mount of Revelation, for our comfort. So we find, *when the enemy cometh in like a flood, the* SPIRIT OF THE LORD *shall lift up a* STANDARD *against him.* The Holy Ghost says, I will stand by and defend the believer in his conflict with corruption and imperfection: only fight the good fight of faith, and victory is infallible. The Standard of holiness and strength always accompanies that of mercy and salvation. And thus the Labarum, which our own Constantine with his whole army saw at York, with this inscription (τύτῳ νίκα), *this Banner must prevail* *, will answer all our wants, and exceed all our expectations.

* The inscription on the cross, which Constantine and all his army saw, was, according to Philostorgius (lib. i. cap. 6.) Ῥωμαίων φωνῇ, *in hoc signo vince:* which Eusebius expresses in Greek, by τύτῳ νίκα· others, as Philostorgius, &c. ἐν τύτῳ νίκα· and that this phænomenon did appear, not to Constantine alone, but also to his army, was affirmed by Constantine upon oath: ὅρκοις πιστωσαμένω τὸν λόγον.—What a proud honour to the British sky, to have exhibited a miraculous omen and assurance, for the establishment and peace of Christianity! What a pledge, if there is faith in history, that this country should be, in a remarkable manner, the seat of religion!

The

[25]

The laſt Banner I ſhall exhibit to your view, is one, of which this ſurrounding audience ſo numerous reminds me. It is that which ſhould never be out of our thoughts, in all our occupations, ſacred and ordinary. It is that, to which the attention of the univerſe will be fixed. It is that, to which thoſe you have already contemplated, ſo ſublime and glorious, are only miniſterial and ſubordinate: namely, that which St. Matthew ſpeaks of, * THE SIGN of the Son of man, appearing in the clouds of heaven, with power and great glory. Jeſus Chriſt Himſelf, conſidered as the great rallying point of heaven, earth, and hell, at the judgment day, is called a *Sign.* Yes! hear, O heavens, and give ear, O earth! A definite time is fixed, when He will *deſcend from heaven with a*

---

* Howſoever part of this 24th chapter primarily means the deſtruction of Jeruſalem, yet Biſhop Newton on the Prophecies, and moſt other commentators, have no doubt, but that the laſt judgment of the world is interwoven with the account of the judgment of Jeruſalem. —Particularly, it is thought, the laſt part of the chapter refers to nothing elſe. And hence in our Bibles the title of the page here is, " Of Chriſt's coming to Judgment."

ſhout

shout (ἐν κελεύσματι), with a *summons* to the whole angelic world, to attend Him: *with the voice of the archangel*, repeating the summons, and *with the trump of God*; a trump so unspeakably sonorous, as to be felt through earth, sea, and skies, and felt by the very dead themselves. The righteous, *the dead in Christ*, shall *revive*, and *rise first: in a moment, in the twinkling of an eye*, shall these be transfigured, and clothed with majestic, beautiful, powerful, luminous, and incorruptible bodies; and then be rapidly borne away in clouds, *to meet the Lord in the air* *. Next, the ungodly shall come out of their graves with frantic amazement, dolorous shrieks, and every circumstance of Fear, and Guilt, and Woe, and Despair; and stand on the ground †, with the Devil and all his angels at their side, or raised, perhaps, *above* them in the air, of which region he was the prince. Jesus Christ supereminent shall be aloft in the midst, surrounded with the human righteous, and all the holy angels. Image to yourselves *three worlds* thus congregated before him: and remember, that you and I shall be

---

* ἁρπαγησόμεθα ἐν νεφέλαις. 1 Thess. iv. 17.
† For only the *righteous* are said to *ascend*.

there; and be parties immediately and individually concerned in the most momentous business of this convention. Though all born of woman will be there, potentates and slaves; philosophers and common understandings; the opulent, and middling ranks, and the poor; judges as well as once their prisoners; priests and people; either sex, of every age, every colour, every quality; still will the transactions of this assembly be as particular, as though every one stood alone upon trial at the bar. The books shall then be opened, the registers by omniscience of all our actions, and words, and thoughts, and hearts. The Judge shall be visible and audible, to hear and answer our several pleas and exceptions *. The righteous shall then be commended, *Well done good and faithful servants;* the wicked shall be dispraised, *Thou wicked and slothful servant:* all minds shall be filled with a sense of the equity of the discrimination: a solemn sentence shall then be pronounced, adjudging the righteous to life eternal, and the ungodly to everlasting punishment. The conflagration

* Lord when saw we &c. And he shall answer, &c. Matt. xxv.

shall then commence from heaven, earth, and hell, about the unrighteous; while the *Holy* ascend with their Judge, Saviour, and Advocate, into the heaven of heavens. There shall they be presented faultless to God the Father *with exceeding joy*, both on His part and theirs. There shall they reside, to exercise their perfect natures in the most noble duties, and to exult in the most transcendent pleasures; in the midst too of a most multitudinous society, where all are majesties, all sages, all splendors, all purities; and where, though all are so many virtues most consummate, yet are all so many sweet, meek, and profound humilities: which blessed state of things is to last, without change, without remission, without intermission, without end; and, what is more, its moral excellence and felicity to be, from the nature of things, ever *augmenting*.—

To conclude. Remember against that day, that IN THE NAME OF OUR GOD *have we set up those Banners*; which, though never called into actual service, have already been, I am happy to say, of use above calculation, in making, at a time like the present, the very imagination of internal tumult impossible: and, besides, in propagating by example zeal for government

ment and love for our country, beyond any thing hitherto known in this, perhaps in any other kingdom.

Your arming, as well as that of the very respectable Cavalry now surrounding us, and that of the counties, towns, villages, and even parishes and corporate bodies of the realm, has also contributed its share to prevent an infuriated invasion of the kingdom, by exhibiting a proof of its total unanimity against the enemy. And, look farther still; *your* arming, conjointly with the whole kingdom arming, will, by intimidating the enemy from future attempts on this realm, tend to secure that peace, perhaps for generations to come, which will gradually diminish our taxes and public burthens, and render us prosperity itself, both in Church and State. Under which considerations, it is impossible you should hereafter remember your present inconvenience or expence: you cheerfully submit to both, in behalf of your present and succeeding selves.

I only add one sentiment more: that, should those Colours be called into awful use, which the last convulsive strokes of an expir-
ing

ing Directory render not impossible; you will remember, that, at the last day, regard will be had to the evidence those Colours will give, of the value you set, not upon the property and lives of yourselves and countrymen, but upon the BIBLE and all RELIGION, here and every where now in danger, and committed this day to the trust of your courage, of your integrity, of your zeal, of your vigilance, and, above all, of your prayers.

FINIS.

Printed by Libri Plureos GmbH in Hamburg, Germany